GREAT BARRIER REEF

AUSTRALIA

PETER LIK

UNDERWATER PHOTOGRAPHY

BOB & DINAH HALSTEAD

"My total dedication and obsession
with photography has taken me
on journeys into many remarkable
areas throughout Australia.
I captured this collection of images
using a specialist panoramic camera.
Because of the wider field of view,
this format enables me to portray
the true spirit of Australia
on film. Upon viewing these images
I am sure you will share with me
the tranquillity and solitude
I experienced whilst exploring the
stunning beauty of this country."

www.peterlikimages.com

PO Box 2529 Cairns Queensland 4870 Australia
Telephone: (07) 4053 9000 **Fax:** (07) 4032 1277
sales@peterlik.com.au   **www.peterlik.com.au**

© **Peter Lik Publishing**   BK01

ISBN 0 646 28248 4

Front cover - Hardy's Lagoon, the Whitsundays
Back cover - Clownfish and anemone

The Great Barrier Reef is Australia's most magnificent natural wonder. This 2,300 kilometre reef stretches from Lady Elliot Island on the Tropic of Capricorn and ends just off the coast of Papua New Guinea. The fragile ecosystem is home for more than 1,500 species of fish, and over 400 different types of coral. There are approximately 2,000 individual reefs ranging in size from one hectare to more than 100 square kilometres forming the Barrier Reef.

Some 600 continental islands and 350 coral cays are dispersed throughout this natural phenomenon. Continental islands are essentially flooded sections of Australia which were isolated from the mainland by the melting of polar ice caps in the ice age approximately 10,000 years ago. Coral cays are formed when sediments from the reef accumulate in a certain area, and build up over years to form fringing reefs and eventually stabilise themselves to provide homes for birdlife and animals.

Although the only living structure on earth to be seen from outer space, the Great Barrier Reef is actually made up of millions of tiny living creatures called polyps which feed on marine organisms in the ocean. There are two different types of coral; hard coral are limestone fortresses which shelter the delicate coral polyps that create reefs. Soft corals, often dazzling with color, extend their nets to sieve food and sway gently in the ocean's currents.

The ultimate way to experience the reef is to snorkel or scuba dive amongst this submersed wonderland. As you descend into the ocean, one immediately discovers the mysteries of these underwater cities. You may encounter a shipwreck, watch a clownfish perform in its magnificent anemone, or catch a glimpse of a shark gliding gracefully by. Every dive holds a new adventure.

To ensure the preservation of this fragile ecosystem, The Great Barrier Reef Marine Park Authority (GBRMPA) was established. To enable future generations to share its beauty, the Reef was declared World Heritage on 26th October, 1981.

We invite you to share the experiences of photographers' Peter Lik and Bob and Dinah Halstead who captured these magnificent images above and below this natural paradise.

Lady Musgrave Island is completely enclosed by a coral lagoon.

This Zebra Lionfish packs a painful sting in its venomous dorsal spines.

A Coral Cod rests beneath a coral crown covered in feather stars.

Chevron Barracuda encircle a lone diver on the Great Barrier Reef.

Previous Page: Birds eye view of Hardys Lagoon.

Starfish of many shapes, colours and sizes inhabit the reef. There are over 350 different species of the Echinoderm discovered on the Great Barrier Reef.

Clownfish protected by its magnificent anemone, into which it quickly retreats at the first sign of danger.

Nudey Beach, Fitzroy Island.

One Tree Island lies south-east of Heron Island.

Lizard Island, a continental island lies 240km north of Cairns.

Low Isles is a pristine coral cay offshore from Port Douglas.
This classic lighthouse over 100 years old still casts its beam over the Coral Sea.

Lady Elliot Island Lighthouse - above twilight and below daybreak.

Lighthouses protect passing ships from shallow reef water. This lighthouse (above) on Lady Elliot Island was built in 1873, and like most other lighthouses on the Great Barrier Reef, was automated in 1988. These majestic beacons guard the 2,300km stretch of reef from Lady Elliot Island in the south, to Boobi Island, the northernmost island in the Torres Straits.

Upolu Cay with the mountains of Cairns in the background.

Seabird's view of sand cay.

*M*ichaelmas and Upolu Cay are pristine sand cays located on the Great Barrier Reef offshore from Cairns. Michaelmas is a vegetated cay and is home for thousands of sea birds. 15kms to the south is Upolu Cay, an island paradise surrounded by magnificent reef.

Sailing around Michaelmas Cay, Great Barrier Reef.

One of the many beautiful coral cays of the Torres Straits.

A juvenile Red Tailed Tropic Bird.

Seabirds including gulls, terns, gannets, sheer waters and frigates all rely on islands and sand cays as important breeding sites. There are 29 species of sea birds that inhabit the Great Barrier Reef. Terns of various species breed on sand cays in very large numbers and over 30,000 may be seen at one time.

Michaelmas Cay, 40km from Cairns is home to over 30,000 birds.

Green Island, a true coral cay 27km offshore from Cairns.

Green Island.

Coral Cays are low islands formed by the buildup of reef sediments. As the reef grows, hardy plants start to flourish in the sand, birds begin to habitate and the vegetated coral cay is then stabilised. The cay then becomes a mini ecosystem amongst the 230,000 square kilometres of the world's largest province, the Great Barrier Reef. There are over 70 named coral cays which are usually surrounded by reef flats. This reef protects the cays from erosion and also provides a great place for snorkelling.

A castaways retreat, Welcome Bay, Fitzroy Island.

*C*ontinental islands such as Fitzroy, Brampton and Orpheus were formed about 10,000 years ago upon the diminishing of the ice age. The melting of polar ice caps caused sea levels to rise and consequently isolated these peaks from the mainland. These islands boast excellent fringing reefs.

Brampton Island National Park.

Twilight over Orpheus Island.

Starfish, brittle stars, sea cucumbers, sea urchins and feather stars are the five creatures which belong to the Echinoderm group found on the Great Barrier Reef. This ancient group of animals has fossil ancestors over 500 million years old. The starfish are common inhabitants of the shallow waters of reef lagoons and are easily located with their bright colours. Their characteristic shape is basically a star with five arms radiating from a central body, which they use to creep along the ocean floor.

Jude enjoys the tropical Coral Sea.

Snorkelling is the most popular activity on the reef.

Square-spot fairy basslet.

Orange-fin anemone fish.

Bird's eye view of Heron Island, Wistari Reef in the background.

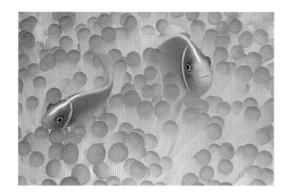

𝒞lownfish on the Great Barrier Reef take refuge inside their magnificent anemone. Although beautiful, the anemone have tentacles which contain lethal stinging cells. These tentacles act as a protector of the anemone fish, and are otherwise poisonous to other species of fish. The distinctive color patterns and dancing motion of these fish make them one of the most entertaining species on the Great Barrier Reef.

Scuba diving is the ultimate way to experience the Great Barrier Reef.

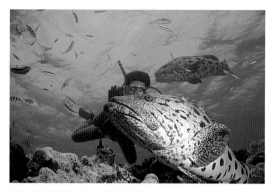

The Cod Hole, Lizard Island.

*C*orals are an amazing group of animals that build the reef. They grow in magnificent shapes, forms and colours, providing shelter and food for its numerous ocean inhabitants. Billions of tiny coral polyps form over 3,000 individual reefs inside this fragile 230,000 square kilometre ecosystem. Some varieties of coral include beautiful fans and whips, fire corals, stag horn, brain, mushroom and organ pipes. The incredible display of coral spawning only occurs for a few nights per year. This is often described as fireworks underwater.

A Bigeye amongst Red Sea Whips.

The swirling silica sands of Hill Inlet -Whitsundays.

Heart Reef - Whitsundays.

Nudey Beach, an isolated cove on Fitzroy Island.

Diving amongst the reef's treasures.

Yellow feather stars sway with the ocean's currents.

Blue sea star in the underwater garden of the coral sea.

The stunning Regal Angelfish flaunts its beautiful colours.

Coconut Palms sway gently over the azure waters of Yorke Island in the Torres Straits.

$\mathcal{D}$olphins are one of the most friendliest inhabitants of the Great Barrier Reef. The bottlenose dolphins enjoy playing in schools, and often ride the bow waves of boats. These beautiful mammals prefer the tepid waters of the reef and grow to about 2 metres. Dolphins are now a protected species.

Tail fluke of the impressive Humpback Whale.

Humpback Whale breach.

A massive whale shark dwarfs a lone diver.

$\mathcal{W}$hales are the largest and most popular mammals to visit the reef waters. The giant humpback whales, which may grow to over 15 metres, spend their winters in the tropics, then travel south for summer feeding in the Antarctic seas. This migration of thousands of kilometres is an annual ritual. The humpback whale is the most vocal of all because they sing a high pitched song underwater. On a calm day, this unusual sound can easily be heard above the ocean's surface. Commercial whaling from 1952 - 1962 reduced the entire population of 10,000 humpbacks migrating on Australia's east coast to 200 whales. After 1962, they were declared a protected species and since then, their population in the Barrier Reef waters has gradually increased to 600. There are two different sub groups of whales; whalebone whales and toothed whales. The whalebone whales strain their food of small plankton from the ocean, whilst the toothed whales are very active predators and swallow their prey of fish and squid whole.

$\mathcal{R}$ays and sharks are perhaps two of the most powerful inhabitants of the reef. The awesome giant manta ray moves gracefully underwater, with strong sweeps of its huge wings weighing about 2 tonnes. Sleek and streamlined, the silvertip shark glides over the reef. This potentially dangerous shark grows up to 3m, and if seen whilst diving should be treated with extreme caution.

The impressive silvertip shark is most likely to be encountered on the Outer Barrier Reef.

Crescent Tail Bigeyes hover in small groups over the deeper reef.

Fire Urchin displays its incandescent colours.

$\mathcal{T}$he Great Barrier Reef marine park, the largest in the world, is situated off the Queensland coast. The availability of qualifying diving courses throughout the islands and coastal areas make it an enviable location for diving. Scuba diving on the reef is relatively easy, and once certified, you can explore the endless coral gardens, thousands of species of fish, shipwrecks and underwater canyons. This experience is possibly one of the world's greatest wilderness adventures.

A young Hawksbill turtle, one of the six species of turtles found on the Great Barrier Reef.

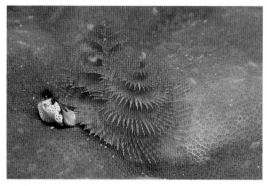

Christmas tree worms burrow into the coral.

Moorish Idols swim in pairs.

A magnificent reef scene.

Mer Island group, the northernmost islands on the Great Barrier Reef.

Shallow sand flats may look like a desert but in fact harbour many marine species that burrow in the sand.

Cabbage coral.

Beautiful corals can be seen close to many isles on the Great Barrier Reef.

Giant sea fans.

Royal Dottyback.

The sea horse is one of the most mysterious creatures to inhabit the reef.

Cape Tribulation - where two World Heritage areas meet, reef and rainforest.

Lady Musgrave Island hosts the perfect lagoon.

Lindeman Island.

$\mathscr{W}$hitsunday group consists of over 70 continental islands; seven of which have resort facilities; Hamilton, Hayman, Lindeman, South Molle, Long, Daydream and Hook. The islands are dispersed on both sides of the Whitsunday passage, within 50 kms of Shute Harbour, the main access to these islands. The Whitsundays offer superb sailing, bareboat charters, snorkelling and diving.

Hayman Island and surrounding reef.

Twilight over Hamilton Island in the Whitsundays.

The virgin white silica sands of Whitehaven; often rated as the world's best beach.

Colourful Feather Stars feed on drifting plankton.

Beaked Coralfish.

*A*ustralia's Great Barrier Reef, surrounded by the tepid waters of the Coral Sea is the largest living structure on earth. This amazing ecosystem is home for 1,500 species of fish, 400 varieties of coral, 4,000 molluscs and other animals. More than 600 islands are dispersed throughout the Barrier Reef; 250 named continental islands and 70 pristine coral cays. These tropical islands are the true version of "paradise" where you can either sleep under the stars or spoil yourself at a five star resort.

The turquoise waters of the Coral Sea embrace the shores of Heron Island.

A Lionfish preys on a multitude of cardinal fishes.

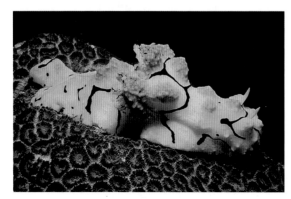

Yellow Nudibranch.

Purple Fairy Basslet.

$\mathcal{A}$ustralia's Great Barrier Reef was gazetted a World Heritage area on 26th October, 1981. The biological and geological complexity of the Reef make it the earth's richest marine habitat. Please take time out to enjoy and preserve this magnificent seventh natural wonder of the world and leave it the way you saw it, so our future generations will also share the splendour and mysteries of the reef.

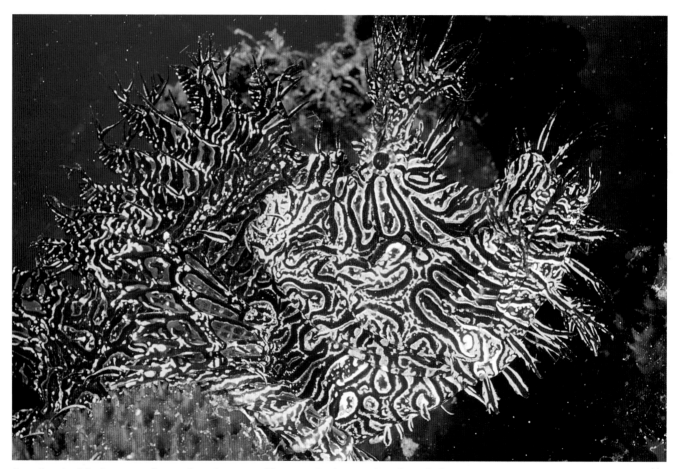

Lacy Scorpionfish, the master of camouflage, disguises itself amongst the glowing colours beneath the ocean.

Anemonefish add to the enchantment of Australia's Great Barrier Reef.

Peter Lik Gallery

Peter Lik, Australia's award-winning panoramic photographer proudly presents his own galleries. His highly successful publishing company, *Peter Lik Publishing*, was born in Cairns just three years ago, providing the marketplace with stylish books and postcards featuring Peter's distinctive imagery.

Signed limited edition prints of Peter's spectacular images are available at the galleries.

Peter Lik Galleries mirror the same enthusiasm and innovative approach to photography as its founder and will continue to expand as a public showcase of Peter's outstanding images.

CAIRNS
4 Shields Street
Tel **(07) 4031 8177**

SYDNEY
QVB, 455 George St
Tel **(02) 9269 0182**

PORT DOUGLAS
19 Macrossan Street
Tel **(07) 4099 6050**

SAN FRANCISCO
Pier 39, Embarcadero
Tel **(415) 765 7515**

www.peterlik.com
info@peterlik.com.au

Books by Peter Lik

- Australia
- Blue Mountains
- Brisbane
- Byron Bay
- Cairns
- Daintree and Cape Tribulation
- Fraser Island
- Gold Coast
- Great Barrier Reef
- Port Douglas
- Sunshine Coast
- Sydney
- The Red Centre
- Townsville and Magnetic Island
- Wildlife
- World Heritage Rainforest
- COLLECTORS EDITION
  "Australia - Images of a Timeless Land"
  (Large format 192 page coffee table book)

 PeterLikPublishing